HOW FAR?

HIGHLIGHTS FOR CHILDREN, INC.

Honesdale, Pennsylvania

Space Q's

Answers on page 36

Planet X?
Can you name the planet shown in each photo?

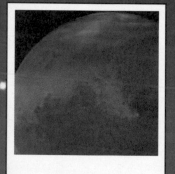

Space Out!

Outer space is home to solar systems, stars, and satellites. It also contains lots of words. Can you make at least 20 words from the letters of OUTER SPACE?

Moon Walk
Can you help this astronaut get back to his ship?

START

FINISH

Illustrated by Mike Dammer

2

Look-Alike Landers

Which two robotic landers are the same?

WELCOME to Gluumgus

The sun never shines on Planet Gluumgus and the rain falls sideways. Draw a picture of an alien who would like living on Gluumgus.

Hey, I can see my house!

Space Dates

Match each of these events to the year it happened.

First man on the moon ●   ●1976

First man in space ●   ●1965

First space walk ●   ●1969

First spacecraft landing on Mars ●   ●1961

3

Got Space?

Renfru is trying to reach his home planet of Xylo by the time the three suns set on it. Can you help him find his way home? Just one path will lead him there. After you've found the way, write down the letters along the path in order from START to FINISH to answer the question below. Now get zooming!

Answer on page 36

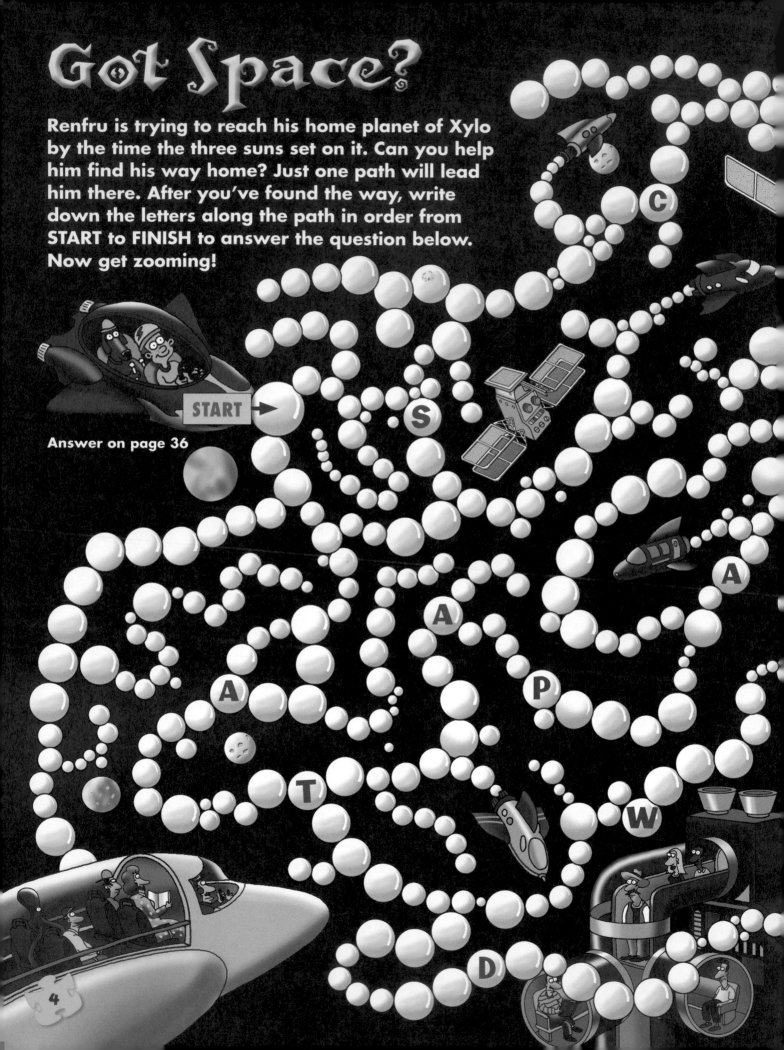

START →

Where will Renfru leave his spaceship when he reaches Xylo?

5, 4, 3, 2, 1...

Inside this rocket are **34** space terms. Your mission is to boldly go up, down, across, backwards, and diagonally. Circle all the words that you find. When you are finished, write the leftover letters in order in the spaces below the rocket. They will give you an important message from mission control.

Answer on page 36

Word List

ARMS	RE-ENTRY
CARGO	BOOSTERS
FORCE	FAIL-SAFE
MOONS	MOMENTUM
ORBIT	MOUNTAIN
SALVO	NOSE CONE
~~APOGEE~~	THRUSTER
ATOMIC	CELESTIAL
COSMOS	ASTRONAUTS
FUNDED	SPLASHDOWN
LANDER	SPACE DEBRIS
RAMJET	CAPE CANAVERAL
RANGER	GUIDANCE SYSTEMS
CAPSULES	MANNED SPACESHIP
CONTROL	ZOOM
MISSION	ZERO
PERIGEE	
NECK-WRENCHING G-FORCES	

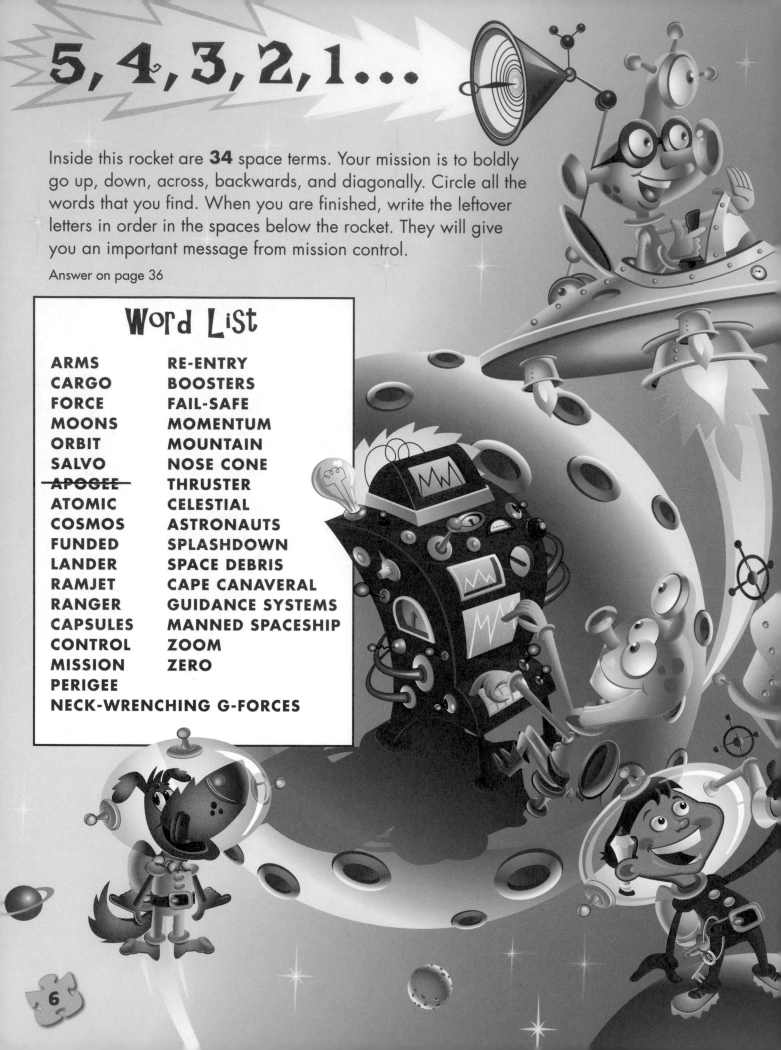

Mission control says, " _ _ _ _ _ _ _ _ _ _ !"

7

UNIDENTIFIED FUNNY OBJECTS

How do astronauts keep their pants up? *They use an asteroid belt.*
If you think that joke is bad, search the galaxy for a better one.
Add your stickers to finish the outer space scene. Then use
the space code to solve the jokes on the next page.

Answer on page 36

UNidENTiFied FuNNy ObjectS Pages 8–9

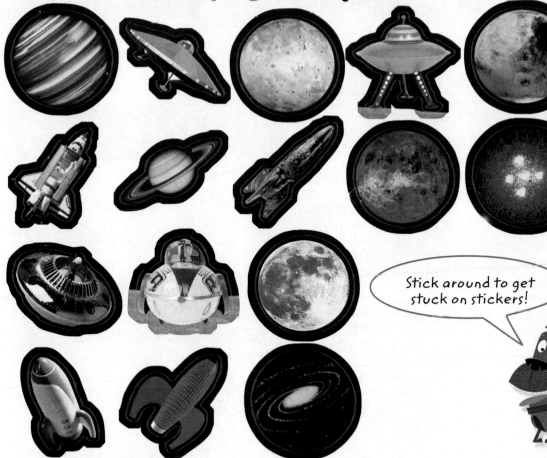

Stick around to get stuck on stickers!

Space Case Pages 16–17

How does the man in the moon cut his hair?

____ - ____ ____ ____ ____ ____ ____ ____ .

What do you call a magician from outer space?

____ ____ ____ ____ ____ ____

____ ____ ____ ____ ____ ____ ____

What do you call a pecan in a spaceship?

____ ____ ____ ____ ____ ____ ____ - ____ ____ ____ ____

How did the rocket lose its job?

____ ____ ____ ____ ____ ____ ____ ____ ____ .

Spaced Out

It's time for Planet Zongo's annual spaceship parade. Folks have come from all over Galaxy Ish to join the fun. But it looks like some bought their spaceships at the same place. Can you find the three pairs of spaceships that match exactly?

Answer on page 37

10

Things Are Heating Up

There is more than meets the eye at this hot-air-balloon festival. Can you find the hidden objects?

Answer on page 37

toothbrush

canoe

shoe

watering can

slice of pie

teacup

open book

sailboat

pencil

slice of pizza

crown

umbrella

ring

banana

bird

fishhook

pen

turtle

carrot

mitten

spatula

kite

comb

golf club

dolphin

13

Roving Robots

Doodad, Widget, and Whorl have rolled to the corners of this maze. But Glitch is stuck in the middle. Can you help Glitch roll to the empty corner?

Answer on page 37

Start

Finish

14

Star Sums

The stars in the Triangulator Galaxy have aligned in a brilliant way. See if you can help them really shine. Fill in each star with one of the numbers from 1 to 19. The three stars that make up the side of each triangle should total 22. No number will appear more than once. We've put in a few numbers to start you off. Fill in the rest, and you are a stellar solver!

Answer on page 37

Space Case

Mission Control just radioed with important information about finding the answer to this riddle. First, use your stickers to finish the picture. Then read each clue to find out which letters to put in which numbered spaces. Ready?
3 . . . 2 . . . 1 . . . Blast off!

Answer on page 37

CLUES

1. Look on the helmet.
2. This letter is riding a shooting star.
3. You will find this letter hanging from the space station.
4. Planet Earth has this letter.
5. This letter is above a flag.
6. Look on the moon.
7. The red planet has this letter.
8. What letter is right between two stars?
9. Look for a letter on a solar panel.
10. You will find this letter on the astronaut's foot.
11. A robotic arm is holding this letter.

What is an astronaut's favorite place on the computer?

___ ___ ___   ___ ___ ___ ___ ___   ___ ___ ___
 1   2   3   4   5   6   7   8   9   10   11

16

Illustrated by Steve Skelton

17

Moonstruck!

We've hidden 19 words or phrases that contain the letters MOON in this grid. Each time MOON appears in a word, it is replaced by ☾. Look up, down, across, backwards, and diagonally to find the words. Now go search by the light of this moon!

Answer on page 37

Answer on page 37

Word List

~~BLUE MOON~~	MOONFACED
CRESCENT MOON	MOONFISH
FULL MOON	MOONFLOWER
HALF-MOON	MOONLIGHT
HARVEST MOON	MOONROOF
HONEYMOON	MOONSCAPE
MAN IN THE MOON	MOON SHOT
MOONBEAM	MOONSTONE
MOON CHILD	MOONWALK
OVER THE MOON	

```
            L  B  Y  C  C
      ☾  T  S  E  V  R  A  H  ☾
   V  ☾  F  A  C  E  D  A  F  F     ☾
   ☾  X  T  ☾  S  ☾  U  X  G  I  E
      I  S  E  S  C  A  S  W  I  S  S     ☾
   O  L  H  T  E  W  ☾  F  L  A  H  H  T  S  L
   G  N  O  N  F  U  L  L  ☾  O  L  H  N  C  U
   E  N  T  M  I  E  R  O  B  B  R  K  I  A  N
   E  ☾  Y  E  N  O  H  V  L  T  E  K  N  P  A
   V  A  P  O  L  L  O  E  U  H  C  A  A  E  R
   ☾  F  L  O  W  E  R  E  G  C  R  M  D
   M  O  K  F  E  T  ☾  I  X  H  N
   C  G  O  ☾  C  H  I  L  D  N  M
   M  J  R  H  E  L  ☾  A  D
      X  ☾  ☾  D  E
```

18

Moon Walk

Twelve men have walked on the moon. Their names can fit in the grid in just one way. Use the number of letters in each person's name as a clue to where it might fit. When you're done, blast to the bottom of the page.

Answer on page 38

Word List

ALAN BEAN 8
JOHN YOUNG 9
BUZZ ALDRIN 10
DAVID SCOTT 10
PETE CONRAD 10
JAMES IRWIN 10
ALAN SHEPARD 11
CHARLES DUKE 11
EUGENE CERNAN 12
NEIL ARMSTRONG 13
EDGAR MITCHELL 13
HARRISON SCHMITT 15

Bonus Puzzle

Unscramble the six shaded letters to spell the name of the space program that sent these men to the moon.

JOHN YOUNG

Puzzle by Lori Mortensen

19

Are You Game?

Sasha is scoring big in Hyper Space Race! Before she wins her game, can you find at least **20** differences between these pictures?

Answer on page 38

20

Which two dance mats match?

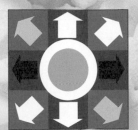 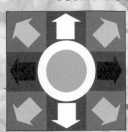  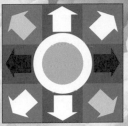 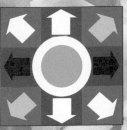

THE GOLF GAME

Illustrated by Dan McGeehan

21

Weather Q's

Answers on page 38

Snow Tread

Charlotte's town is covered in snow! Can you help her find the one path home from school?

School

Start

Finish

Illustrated by Mike Moran   Puzzles by Carly Schuna

Weather Quiz

Which of these weather facts are true and which are false?

1. The longest lightning bolt ever recorded was nearly 120 miles long.

T or F

2. The hottest temperature ever recorded on the earth was in New Mexico.

T or F

3. The coldest temperature ever recorded on Earth was -50 degrees Fahrenheit.

T or F

4. The strongest wind gust ever recorded on the earth's surface was in New Hampshire.

T or F

Wacky Weather

Explorers have just discovered Climatopia—a place that has all four seasons on the same block! Draw a scene from Climatopia here.

Cloud Gazing

Three of these words are types of clouds, and the others are fakers. Can you circle the clouds?

RUMPUS

DIPLODOCUS

NIMBUS

ONUS

ABACUS

STRATUS

ESOPHAGUS HIBISCUS

CUMULUS

It's Raining, It's Pouring

Which two umbrellas match exactly?

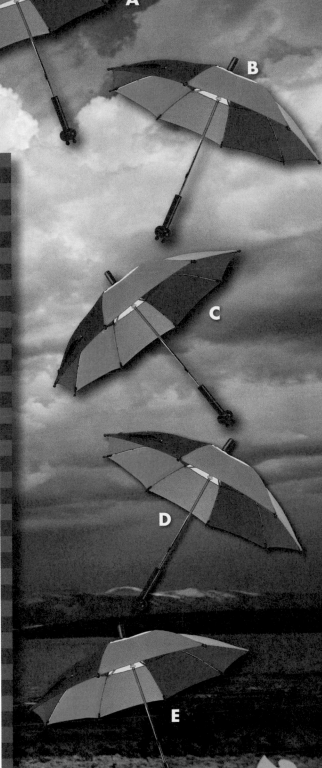

Weather Words

Meteorology is the study of weather and forecasting. It includes a huge number of topics—and a lot of words, too. Can you make at least **20** words from the letters in **METEOROLOGY**?

_____ _____
_____ _____
_____ _____
_____ _____
_____ _____
_____ _____
_____ _____
_____ _____
_____ _____
_____ _____

Scrambled Space

Need more space? You've come to the right place! Unscramble these space words. Once you have them all straightened out, read down the column of boxes to learn the answer to this riddle:

What do you get when you cross a galaxy and a toad?

Answer on page 38

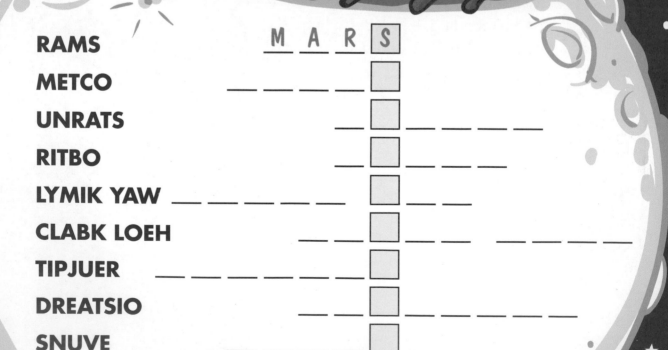

RAMS   M A R [S]

METCO   _ _ _ _ [ ]

UNRATS   _ [ ] _ _ _

RITBO   _ [ ] _ _ _

LYMIK YAW   _ _ _ _ [ ] _ _ _

CLABK LOEH   _ _ _ [ ] _ _ _ _

TIPJUER   _ _ _ [ ] _ _ _

DREATSIO   _ _ [ ] _ _ _ _

SNUVE   _ _ [ ] _ _

Illustrated by Dave Clegg

24

Stick around to get stuck on stickers!

You're seeing stars!

Use these stickers to mark your favorite puzzles— or anything else you like.

Mania®

Highlights™

PuzzleMania®

Pu

ights™

PuzzleMania®

Highlights™

Pu

Mania®

Highlights™

PuzzleMania®

M

ights™

PuzzleMania®

Highlights™

Pu

Mania®

Highlights™

PuzzleMania®

M

ights™

PuzzleMania®

Highlights™

Pu

Mania®

Highlights™

PuzzleMania®

M

ights™

PuzzleMania®

Highlights™

Pu

Mania®

Highlights™

PuzzleMania®

H

ights™

PuzzleMania®

Highlights™

Pu

Space Sudoku

Use your stickers to finish this puzzle. When you are done, each row, column, and little grid must contain one of each kind of planet, sun, or moon.

Answer on page 39

Double Cross

Can you shed some light on this puzzle? To find the answer to the riddle below, first cross out all the pairs of matching letters. Then write the remaining letters in order in the spaces beneath the riddle.

Answer on page 39

SS	BB	LL	IM	QQ	CC	TT
VE	DD	XX	EE	OO	RY	JJ
NN	WW	II	PL	ZZ	AA	KK
UU	EA	SS	LL	HH	OO	SE
RR	DD	DT	VV	EE	II	MM
YY	UU	OO	OH	PP	CC	EA
GG	TT	TY	AA	KK	OU	EE

What did the sun say when it was introduced to Earth?

_ ' _ _ _ _ _

_ _ _ _ _ _ _

_ _ _ _ _ _ .

26

Hidden Pairs

Each pair of words below is hiding something. Look closely and you'll find a pair of shorter but related words in the original pair. For example, in the first pair you can find **MOM** and **DAD**. Can you find the other hidden pairs?

Answer on page 39

1. **mom**ent, doo**dad**

2. struck, cargo

3. badger, goodbye

4. diving, shout

5. charm, bubblegum

6. history, sherbet

7. clover, thunder

8. sunken, honeymoon

9. grunt, boardwalk

10. rocket, stroll

11. frightened, leftovers

12. shower, constellation

Illustrated by Kelly Kennedy

HOME SWEET HOME

Zig, Vot, and Spo are homesick. Use the clues to help each of them get back to the right planet on the right spaceship.

Answer on page 39

Use the chart to keep track of your answers.
Put an **X** in each box that can't be true and an **⬤** in boxes that match.

	Hot Planet	Cold Planet	Wet Planet	Red Ship	Yellow Ship	Blue Ship
Zig						
Vot						
Spo						

CLUES:
1. The red spaceship came from a hot planet.
2. Vot's planet is cold, but not wet.
3. The yellow spaceship belongs to Spo.

Illustrated by Jim Steck

Reading Space

Do you know what astronauts like to read? Follow each line from a letter to a blank space and write the letter in that space. When you are finished, you will have the answer.

Answer on page 39

Illustrated by Mike Moran

Yolanda's screen saver is out of this world! There are three pairs of space creatures that match exactly. Can you find all three pairs?

Answer on page 39

Illustrated by Garry Colby

Here Comes the SUN!

Grab your sunglasses! We've hidden **35** words or phrases that contain the letters *SUN* in this grid. Each time SUN appears in a word, it is replaced by a ☀. Look up, down, across, backwards, and diagonally to find the words. If you can find them all, you are a star!

Answer on page 40

Word List

MIDNIGHT SUN

SUNBATHE

SUNBEAM

SUN BEAR

SUNBELT

SUNBLOCK

SUNBONNET

SUNBURN

SUNBURST

SUNDAE

SUN DANCE

SUNDAY

SUNDEW

SUNDIAL

SUNDOWN

SUNDRESS

SUNFISH

SUNFLOWER

SUNGLASSES

SUNHAT

SUNLAMP

SUNLIGHT

SUNNY-SIDE-UP

SUNPORCH

SUNRISE

SUNROOF

SUNSCREEN

SUNSEEKER

SUNSET

SUNSHINE

SUNSPOT

SUNSTROKE

SUNSUIT

SUNTAN

SUNUP

Tic Tac Row

Each of these spaceships has something in common with the other two spaceships in the same row. For example, in the first row across all three spaceships have antennae on top. Look at the other rows across, down, and diagonally. Can you tell what's alike in each row?

Answer on page 40

34

Illustrated by Jim Paillot

Each of these robots has something in common with the other two robots in the same row. For example, in the first row across all three robots are on wheels. Look at the other rows across, down, and diagonally. Can you tell what's alike in each row?

Answer on page 40

Illustrated by Dave Clegg

ANSWERS

2-3 Space Q's

Planet X?

Saturn   Jupiter

Mars   Earth

Space Out!

Here are 21 words we found. You may have found others.

or	cat	eat	rot	toe	stop	user
so	cup	oar	sea	top	tree	sport
up	ear	rat	see	use	true	carpet

Moon Walk

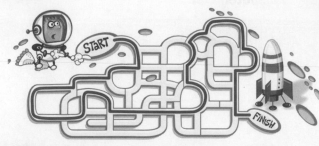

Look-Alike Landers

Space Dates

First man on the moon 1969
First man in space 1961
First space walk 1965
First spacecraft landing on Mars..........1976

4-5 Got Space?

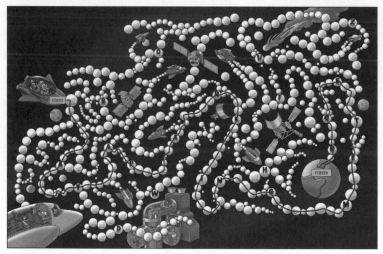

Where will Renfru leave his spaceship when he reaches Xylo?
AT A PARKING METEOR

8-9 Unidentified Funny Objects

How does the man in the moon cut his hair?
E-CLIPSE IT.

What do you call a magician from outer space?
A FLYING SORCERER

What do you call a pecan in a spaceship?
AN ASTRO-NUT

How did the rocket lose its job?
IT GOT FIRED.

6-7 5, 4, 3, 2, 1...

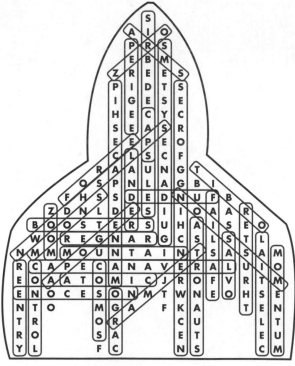

Mission control says, "BLAST OFF!"

36

10–11 Spaced Out

12–13 Things Are Heating Up

14 Roving Robots

15 Star Sums

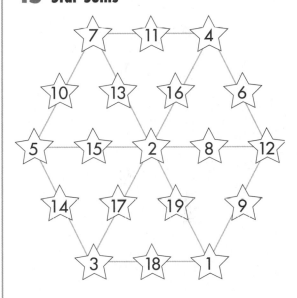

16–17 Space Case

What is an astronaut's favorite place
on the computer?
THE SPACE BAR

18 Moonstruck!

37

ANSWERS

19 Moon Walk

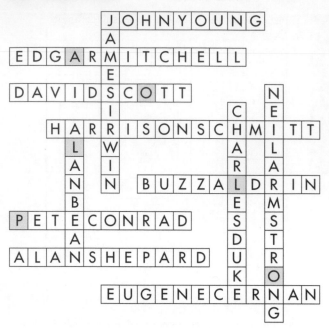

The space program's name was APOLLO.

20–21 Are You Game?

22–23 Weather Q's

Snow Tread

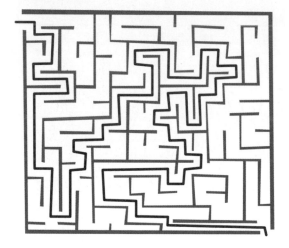

Weather Quiz

1. True
2. False. The world's highest recorded temperature was in Libya: 134 degrees Fahrenheit in 1922.
3. False. It was -128 degrees Fahrenheit recorded in Antarctica in 1983.
4. True. It was 231 miles an hour recorded in 1934 on the top of Mount Washington.

Weather Words

Here are some words we found. You may have found others.

get	moor
greet	more
leg	ore
let	role
log	room
lore	tee
meet	toy
melt	yet
met meteor	yore
mole	

It's Raining, It's Pouring

B and C are exactly alike.

Cloud Gazing

NIMBUS, CUMULUS, and STRATUS are the clouds.

24 Scrambled Space

RAMS	MARS
METCO	COMET
UNRATS	SATURN
RITBO	ORBIT
LYMIK YAW	MILKY WAY
CLABK LOEH	BLACK HOLE
TIPJUER	JUPITER
DREATSIO	ASTEROID
SNUVE	VENUS

What do you get when you cross a galaxy and a toad?
STAR WARTS

25 Space Sudoku

26 Double Cross

What did the sun say when it was introduced to Earth?
"I'm very pleased to heat you."

27 Hidden Pairs

1. mom, dad
2. truck, car
3. bad, good
4. in, out
5. arm, leg
6. his, her
7. over, under
8. sun, moon
9. run, walk
10. rock, roll
11. right, left
12. show, tell

28 Home Sweet Home

Zig: hot planet and red ship
Vot: cold planet and blue ship
Spo: wet planet and yellow ship

29 Reading Space

30–31 Screen Scene

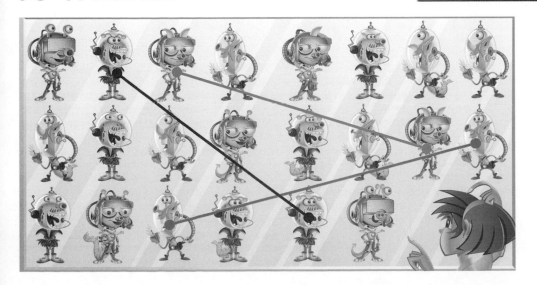

39

ANSWers

32–33 Here Comes the Sun!

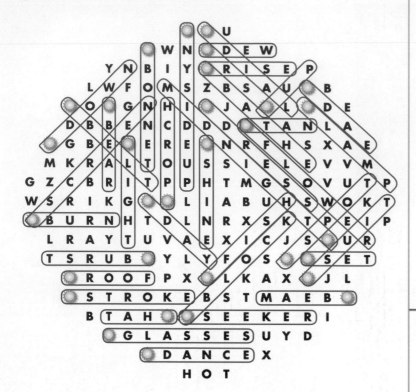

34 Tic Tac Row

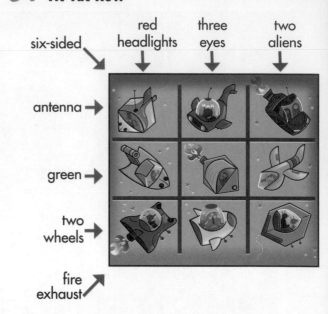

35 Tic Tac Row

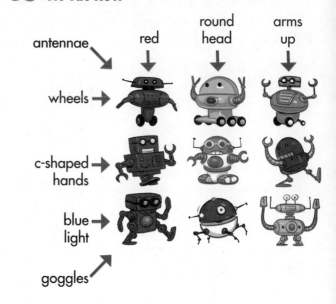